VEGAN

5 INGREDIENTS

Quick and easy, delicious, plant based recipes in 30 minutes or less.

CookNation

I0177819

VEGAN 5 INGREDIENTS
QUICK AND EASY, DELICIOUS, PLANT BASED RECIPES IN 30 MINUTES OR LESS

ISBN 978-1-913174-08-8

DISCLAIMER

CONTENTS

LENTILS, GRAINS AND PASTA 51

DESSERTS   73

CONVERSION CHART   95

INTRODUCTION

The benefits of a plant-based diet are extensive and range from saving you money to boosting your energy levels and improving your health.

Life is pretty fast paced these days, more so than ever before. We're all trying to achieve the impossible, fitting in more tasks throughout the working day and moving at double speed. More often than not, our priorities shift in order to accommodate this busy, and sometimes chaotic, lifestyle. Sadly diet, nutrition and cooking are the first things that westerners seem to leave at the wayside. Of course, it is easy to see why when many fast, on-the-go options are now so readily available and tempting to us. Whether grabbing a microwave meal off the shelf, or having your preferred cuisine delivered to your front door by super-speedy moped, fast food has quietly crept from being a 'one off' or 'weekend treat' to an often daily occurrence for some, compromising our health by making us choose between nutrition and convenience.

Whilst this is not news to most, it is only in recent years that we have really begun to understand the true consequences of such a convenience based diet: food grown, processed and cooked at warp speed. Our body is not built to process this 'fast', and often mass-produced food and attempts to manage it by either eradicating the contents from our system as quickly as possible, resulting in upset stomachs, or by turning it into excess fat on the hips and abdomen. Either way, this is harmful to our digestive system and overall health.

Thankfully though, the focus is now shifting back to real, high quality whole foods; people want to know more about what they're eating, including the nutritional content, use of additives and preservatives and its ecological, ethical and environmental impact.

More recently, there have been a distinct rise in the number of conscious cooks and diners. From farm to fork: how has this food reached my plate? Is the process sustainable? Am I happy with the process? How will this food affect my body? These are just a few questions that growing numbers of the population have been asking, and has led to many people adopting a plant-based diet.

Although many of the early supporters of the plant-based diet were focussed on the ethical side, many people now gravitate towards this lifestyle for its many health benefits. Plant-based diets can have a phenomenal impact on your body, from improving and regulating the digestive system, to enabling effective and healthy weight loss and management.

So, what is a plant-based diet? A common misconception is that those who follow a plant-based diet sit down to a bowl of leaves for each meal, nibbling on lettuce and broccoli, with the odd carrot thrown in for crunch. But you'll be pleased to know that this is far from the truth. A plant-based diet typically follows the same concepts as veganism, no meat or fish is consumed, and other animal products, such as milk, eggs and honey, are also eliminated. Many people use plant-based diet principles as a tool to gradually scale down their intake of meat, fish and animal products. This selection of wonderfully delicious plant-based recipes is suitable for anyone, whether you're planning to adopt a fully plant-based diet, or just want to dip your toes in the water – it is up to you how often you choose to use the ideas in this cookbook. From 'meat-free Monday' to a 24/7 plant-based lifestyle, the choice is entirely yours.

The benefits of a plant-based diet are extensive and range from saving you money to boosting your energy levels and improving your health. One of the most common drivers for switching to a plant-based diet is the concept of 'clean eating'. Mass-produced meat and animal products are usually of poor quality, even by UK standards, with animals often over-fed and over-medicated to ensure they grow quickly - ready-to-be-sold for consumption -profits being the core focus. Farming ethics aside, the health ramifications of consuming mass produced animal products can be significant - overly processed meats can drastically impact digestion, slowing your system down and clogging it up. Over time, this can lead to more problematic digestive issues, such as IBS, bloating, irregular bowel movements and abdominal discomfort. With this, comes a feeling of sluggishness, a lack of energy and, often, weight gain.

Opting for a plant-based diet puts you back in control of your meals, quite literally going back to basics and re-educating yourself on not just the incredible variety of vegetables, pastas, grains, lentils, spices and flavours that this diet can offer, but understanding just how much healthier they can make you feel. These natural products can re-boot your digestive system, flooding your body with the essential nutrients, antioxidants, minerals and vitamins it needs to stabilise your energy levels and enable your digestive and immune systems to perform most effectively.

A diet rich in vegetables, lentils, grains and fruits can drastically aid existing health conditions, as well as help to prevent the development of medical issues later in life. One of the most significant health benefits of plant-focussed eating is the improved ability to control your weight, and maintain a healthy body mass index.

Understanding the impact our diet and lifestyle has on our physical and mental health is incredibly important. Educating ourselves about our food, where it comes from and how it affects our bodies will not only improve our lives now, but help to preserve our health in the future . By eliminating animal products, avoiding artificial preservatives and additives, and eliminating processed foods such as takeaways and microwave meals, and instead gravitating towards a plant-based diet can substantially improve our physical appearance and mental health, as well as boosting the digestive system, immune system and increase energy levels.

International influences and imports have allowed us to fill up our plates with fabulous flavours and an unbelievable variety of options. It may seem intimidating to cook without animal products, so we have put together this beginner's guide to plant-based cooking with some simple, yet delicious, recipes that can be thrown together by even the most inexperienced or apprehensive cooks.

We understand that you may rarely have hours to spend in the kitchen, or the patience, not to mention the budget, to source lots of different ingredients for one meal. With that in mind, every single recipe in this collection has no more than five additional ingredients, alongside some staple store cupboard essentials, and most can be cooked in 30 minutes or less. So now is the time to clear out your cupboards and start filling them with essential products that you will use every day. To help, we have compiled a short list of products that underpin many of the recipes in this book. Once you have these in items your cupboard, you will never need more than five other ingredients to whip up great plant based meals, salads, sides, snacks & desserts..

STORE CUPBOARD ITEMS

- Olive oil
- Coconut oil
- Sunflower oil
- Sea salt
- Black pepper
- Lemon juice
- Tinned tomatoes
- Tomato puree
- Balsamic vinegar
- Vinegar

- Chilli powder
- Mild chilli powder
- Paprika
- Garlic
- Light brown sugar
- Plain flour
- Self-raising flour
- Baking soda
- Caster sugar
- Vanilla extract

Enjoy!

RAW AND ROASTED

Salads

AVOCADO AND MASHED MANGO SALAD

V5

5 Ingredients

- 1 small, ripe mango, peeled, de-stoned and chopped
- 1 avocado, peeled, de-stoned and chopped
- 100g/3½oz baby leaf salad
- ½ tsp sesame seeds
- ½ tsp chia seeds

Method

1 Pour 1 tablespoon of olive oil into a small bowl.

2 Add in ½ teaspoon of lemon juice, season with sea salt and black pepper, and stir well.

3 Place the chopped mango in a separate bowl.

4 Using a pestle, or the end of a wooden rolling pin, give the mango a light bashing, so that the chunks begin to soften, but not so much that they begin to completely break down.

5 Drain some of the mango juice into the olive oil mixture to make the dressing – stir and set to one side.

6 If there is a lot of mango juice remaining, drain and discard.

7 Add the chopped avocado and salad leaves to the mango and toss well.

8 Drizzle in some of the dressing, along with the seeds, and toss well once more.

9 Serve with the remaining dressing on the side.

WHAT YOU'LL NEED FROM YOUR STORE CUPBOARD
•Olive oil•Lemon juice•Sea salt and black pepper

ROASTED BEETROOT AND SUPER SEED SALAD

V5

5 Ingredients

- 1 small beetroot, peeled and chopped
- 150g/5oz baby leaf salad
- 1 tsp pumpkin seeds
- 1 tsp chia seeds
- 1 tsp pine nuts

Method

1 Preheat the oven to 200C/400F/Gas Mark 6.

2 Add the chopped beetroot to a bowl and drizzle over some olive oil.

3 Toss the beetroot in the oil to ensure an even coating, season with a good pinch of sea salt, and place onto a roasting tray.

4 Roast in the oven for 20-25 minutes, or until the beetroot is tender and beginning to crisp.

5 Place the salad leaves in a bowl.

6 Once cooked, place the roasted beetroot into the salad bowl, along with any of the excess oil and juices to use as a salad dressing.

7 Sprinkle in the seeds and nuts, toss well and serve whilst still warm.

WHAT YOU'LL NEED FROM YOUR STORE CUPBOARD
•Olive oil•Sea salt

TOMATO AND AUBERGINE SALAD

V5

5 Ingredients

- 1 aubergine, chopped
- ½ courgette, chopped
- 100g/3½oz cherry tomatoes, halved
- ½ red onion, peeled and chopped
- 75g/3oz rocket leaves

Method

1 Preheat the oven to 180C/350F/Gas Mark 4.

2 Place the chopped vegetables into a bowl and drizzle over some olive oil.

3 Crush 1 clove of garlic into the bowl, add in a good pinch of sea salt, and toss well with the vegetables to ensure an even coating.

4 Transfer into a roasting dish and place in the oven for 20-25 minutes, stirring half way through and making sure everything is tender and golden before removing from the oven.

5 Once cooked, place into a bowl with the rocket leaves.

6 Drizzle over some balsamic vinegar, toss well and serve.

WHAT YOU'LL NEED FROM YOUR STORE CUPBOARD
•Olive oil•Garlic•Sea salt•Balsamic vinegar

POTATO AND GREEN BEAN SUPER SALAD

V5

5 Ingredients

- 75g/3oz new potatoes
- 75g/3oz green beans, chopped
- 75g/3oz mangetout
- 75g/3oz broad beans
- 1 tbsp cashew nuts, crushed

Method

1 Bring a pan of water to boil.

2 Meanwhile, mix 1 tablespoon of olive oil with ½ clove of freshly minced garlic to make a simple dressing. Add in a pinch of black pepper, stir well and set aside.

3 Place the new potatoes in the pan and boil for 12 minutes.

4 Next, add in the green beans and mangetout and simmer for a further 5 minutes, or until everything is tender.

5 Then, add in the broad beans for a further 2-3 minutes just to warm through.

6 Once the vegetables are cooked, drain and transfer into a bowl.

7 Drizzle over the prepared dressing and toss well.

8 Sprinkle over the chopped cashew nuts and serve whilst still warm.

WHAT YOU'LL NEED FROM YOUR STORE CUPBOARD
•Olive oil•Garlic

ROASTED BEETROOT AND LENTIL SALAD

V5

5 Ingredients

- 500g/1lb 2oz beetroot, diced
- 2 red onions, cut into wedges
- 300g/11oz lentils
- A handful of fresh coriander, finely chopped
- 50g/2oz pine nuts

Method

1 Preheat the oven to 400F/200C/Gas Mark 6.

2 Place the beetroot and onions on a roasting tray, drizzle over some olive oil, season with sea salt, and roast for 20-25 minutes, or until the beetroot is tender.

3 Meanwhile, pour the lentils into a small saucepan and cover them with cold water.

4 Bring the pan to the boil and cook for 20 minutes, or until tender, then drain and set aside.

5 Add the roasted beetroot, red onions, lentils, 1 tablespoon of balsamic vinegar and the chopped coriander into a large serving bowl and toss well before serving.

6 Serve warm with a scattering of pine nuts on top.

WHAT YOU'LL NEED FROM YOUR STORE CUPBOARD
•Olive oil •Sea salt •Balsamic vinegar

ASPARAGUS AND BEAN SALAD

V5

5 Ingredients

- 150g/5oz asparagus, tough ends removed
- 400g/14oz tinned cannellini beans, rinsed and drained
- 100g/3½oz spinach, washed
- 200g/7oz sundried tomatoes
- Zest of 1 lemon, grated

Method

1 Preheat a saucepan of water on a medium heat.

2 When the water begins to boil, place the asparagus on top in a steamer and cook for 5 minutes, or until al dente.

3 Meanwhile, mix the cannellini beans, spinach, sundried tomatoes and a pinch of black pepper together in a bowl.

4 Place the cooked asparagus in the bowl, along with the lemon zest and 1 teaspoon of lemon juice.

5 Toss well and enjoy straight away.

WHAT YOU'LL NEED FROM YOUR STORE CUPBOARD
•Black pepper•Lemon juice

KALE AND SWEET POTATO SALAD

V5

5 Ingredients

- 2 sweet potatoes, peeled and diced
- 400g/14oz baby kale
- 100g/3½oz red cabbage, finely chopped
- 75g/3oz cherry tomatoes, halved
- 50g/2oz pine nuts

Method

1 Preheat the oven to 350F/180C/Gas Mark 4.

2 Drizzle some olive oil over the sweet potato chunks and season with sea salt.

3 Place the sweet potato on a baking tray and roast for 20–25 minutes, or until the flesh is tender.

4 Remove any thick stems from the kale and chop only the tender leaves.

5 Add the chopped kale leaves, red cabbage and cherry tomatoes to a bowl and mix well.

6 Add in the pine nuts and ½ tablespoon of balsamic vinegar. Toss well to get an even coating.

7 To serve, divide the salad between two plates and place the sweet potatoes on top.

8 Sprinkle over any remaining pine nuts and serve.

WHAT YOU'LL NEED FROM YOUR STORE CUPBOARD
•Olive oil•Sea salt•Balsamic vinegar

CUCUMBER, MINT AND PINE NUT SALAD

V5

5 Ingredients

- 1 tbsp lime juice, freshly squeezed
- 2 tsp fresh mint leaves, very finely chopped
- 250g/4oz baby leaf salad
- 1 cucumber, cut into ribbons or thin strips
- 1 tbsp pine nuts

Method

1 Mix 3 tablespoon of olive oil, the lime juice and mint together in a small container.

2 Use a blender to blitz together so that the mint leaves begin to liquidise.

3 If the dressing is thickening too much, add in a splash of water.

4 Place the salad leaves in a bowl and drizzle over half of the mint dressing.

5 Toss well, then transfer onto plates ready to serve as the salad base.

6 Arrange the cucumber ribbons on top and drizzle over a little more of the minty salad dressing.

7 Sprinkle over the pine nuts and serve.

WHAT YOU'LL NEED FROM YOUR STORE CUPBOARD
- Olive oil

ROASTED VEGETABLE SALAD

V5

5 Ingredients

- 1 small red onion, peeled and chopped
- 1 red bell pepper, de-seeded and chopped
- 1 yellow bell pepper, de-seeded and chopped
- ½ courgette, chopped
- 2 large tomatoes, chopped

Method

1 Preheat the oven to 350F/180C/Gas Mark 4.

2 Place the chopped vegetables in a roasting dish and generously drizzle over some olive oil.

3 Season with a good pinch of sea salt and black pepper and stir, ensuring an even coating.

4 Roast in the oven for 20–25 minutes, or until tender.

5 Remove from the oven and leave to rest for 2-3 minutes.

6 Transfer the roasted vegetables into a bowl and drizzle over a splash of balsamic vinegar.

7 Season with a pinch of sea salt and black pepper, add a splash of lemon juice, toss the salad well and serve.

WHAT YOU'LL NEED FROM YOUR STORE CUPBOARD

•Olive oil•Sea salt and black pepper
•Balsamic vinegar

ORANGE AND CHILLI SALAD

V5

5 Ingredients

- 1 tsp freshly squeezed orange juice
- 1 red chilli, de-seeded and finely sliced
- ½ onion, peeled and chopped
- 100g/3½oz rocket leaf salad
- 1 orange, peeled and segmented

Method

1 Pour the freshly squeezed orange juice into a small bowl to use for the dressing.

2 Add in 1 tablespoon of olive oil and a pinch of black pepper and stir well.

3 Toss the red chilli, onion and rocket leaves together in a bowl.

4 Pour over some of the prepared dressing and toss the salad once more.

5 Spoon the dressed salad into bowls to serve.

6 Arrange the orange segments on top of the salad, drizzle over a splash more dressing and serve.

WHAT YOU'LL NEED FROM YOUR STORE CUPBOARD

•Olive oil•Black pepper

TOFU, FENNEL AND LINSEED SALAD

V5

5 Ingredients

- 200g/7oz firm tofu, chopped
- 1 fennel bulb, finely chopped
- 1 red onion, peeled and roughly chopped
- 2 large handfuls of fresh rocket leaves
- 2 tsp linseeds

Method

1 Add 2 tablespoon of olive oil to 1 teaspoon of lemon juice, along with a pinch of black pepper, and mix well.

2 Place a pan on a medium heat and add in a splash of coconut oil.

3 Gently press the tofu on a kitchen towel to remove any excess moisture.

4 Add the tofu to the pan and cook for 5-7 minutes, turning half way through.

5 Place the chopped fennel, onion and rocket leaves into a bowl and toss well.

6 Drizzle over some of the prepared salad dressing and toss well, before spooning into bowls to serve.

7 Once cooked, add the tofu onto the salad straight from the pan.

8 Drizzle over a splash more dressing and sprinkle over the linseeds to serve.

WHAT YOU'LL NEED FROM YOUR STORE CUPBOARD
•Olive oil•Lemon juice•Black pepper•Coconut oil

CUCUMBER, AVOCADO AND LIME SALAD

V5

5 Ingredients

- 1 lime, zest and juice
- 1 tsp fresh coriander, finely chopped
- ½ cucumber, finely chopped
- 1 avocado, peeled, de-stoned and chopped
- 1 large handful fresh baby leaf salad

Method

1 Mix 1 teaspoon of olive oil together with a good splash of freshly squeezed lime juice.

2 Add in a pinch of freshly chopped coriander, mix well, and set aside to dress the salad shortly.

3 Place the chopped cucumber and avocado in a bowl, with the baby leaf salad, and toss well.

4 Grate in the zest of half of the lime, squeeze in a splash more lime juice, then drizzle in some of the prepared dressing.

5 Toss well and garnish with some of the remaining coriander to serve.

WHAT YOU'LL NEED FROM YOUR STORE CUPBOARD
- Olive oil

ENGLISH GARDEN SALAD

V5

5 Ingredients

- ½ iceberg lettuce, chopped
- ¼ cucumber, chopped
- 1 radish, finely sliced
- 1 spring onion, finely sliced
- 1 handful of cherry tomatoes, halved

Method

1 Place the chopped lettuce into a bowl along with the cucumber and toss.

2 Add in the radish and spring onion, and combine.

3 Add in the tomatoes and toss once more, ready to serve.

4 Drizzle over a splash of olive oil, add in a small dash of lemon juice and enjoy.

WHAT YOU'LL NEED FROM YOUR STORE CUPBOARD
•Olive oil•Lemon juice

PUMPKIN AND TOFU SALAD

V5

5 Ingredients

- 150g/5oz pumpkin, peeled and diced
- 100g/3oz rocket leaves
- 1 avocado, peeled, de-stoned and chopped
- 150g/5oz tofu, sliced
- 1 tsp pine nuts

Method

1 Preheat the oven to 400F/200C/Gas Mark 6.

2 Place the pumpkin chunks on a roasting tray and drizzle over some olive oil. Sprinkle over some sea salt to season and gently toss to evenly coat.

3 Roast in the oven for 20-25 minutes or until tender..

4 Meanwhile, toss the salad leaves and avocado together in a bowl. Drizzle over a little olive oil and a splash of lemon juice. Toss well once more and set aside.

5 Place a frying pan on a medium heat and allow the pan to warm.

6 Dry cook the tofu for 2–3 minutes, or until it starts to 'sweat', then turn and repeat on the other side.

7 Once cooked, remove the pumpkin from the oven, transfer into the bowl of salad leaves, and gently toss together.

8 Spoon the pumpkin salad onto plates to serve. Add the cooked tofu, straight from the pan, and sprinkle over the pine nuts.

9 Serve and enjoy whilst still warm.

WHAT YOU'LL NEED FROM YOUR STORE CUPBOARD
•Olive oil•Sea salt•Lemon juice

SPICY CHICKPEA SALAD

V5

5 Ingredients

- 200g/7oz tinned chickpeas, drained and rinsed
- 150g/5oz tinned chopped tomatoes
- 1 tbsp tomato puree
- 1 red chilli, de-seeded and finely sliced
- 100g/3½oz rocket leaves

Method

1 Place the chickpeas and chilli into a bowl and add the tinned chopped tomatoes.

2 Add in a freshly minced clove of garlic, ½ teaspoon of lemon juice, ½ teaspoon of balsamic vinegar, then season with sea salt and black pepper,

3 Spoon in the tomato puree and 1 teaspoon of chilli powder (or to taste).

4 Mix well and transfer the contents to a small pan.

5 Allow the mixture to simmer on a low heat for 3-5 minutes, stirring occasionally, until the mixture reduces slightly.

6 If it's still watery, continue to simmer for a few more minutes.

7 Remove from the heat and serve over a bed of fresh rocket leaves.

WHAT YOU'LL NEED FROM YOUR STORE CUPBOARD

Garlic•Lemon juice •Balsamic vinegar•Sea salt and black pepper •Chilli powder

NICE AND SIMPLE POTATO SALAD

V5

5 Ingredients

- 125g/4oz new potatoes, halved
- 1 tbsp dairy-free Greek style yoghurt
- 2 spring onions, finely slices
- ½ red onion, peeled and finely chopped
- Pinch fresh parsley, finely chopped

Method

1 Bring a pan of water to boil and add in the new potatoes with a splash of olive oil.

2 Cook for 15-20 minutes, until tender.

3 Drain and return the potatoes to the pan.

4 Spoon in the Greek-style yoghurt and season with a pinch of sea salt and black pepper.

5 Gently mix the potatoes in the yoghurt, adding a little more if required.

6 Add in the spring onion and red onion, mixing well once more, but being careful not to break up the potatoes.

7 Garnish with freshly chopped parsley and either serve whilst still warm, or allow to cool and then refrigerate to eat chilled later on.

WHAT YOU'LL NEED FROM YOUR STORE CUPBOARD
•Olive oil•Sea salt and black pepper

BEETROOT AND BALSAMIC SALAD

V5

5 Ingredients

- 1 beetroot, peeled and chopped
- 150g/5oz baby leaf salad
- 75g/3oz cucumber, sliced and quartered
- ½ red onion, peeled and finely chopped
- 50g/2oz pomegranate seeds

Method

1 Preheat the oven to 200C/400F/Gas Mark 6.

2 Wrap the beetroot in tin foil and place on a roasting tray.

3 Cook in the oven for 25-30 minutes, or until tender.

4 Remove from the oven, carefully peel back some of the tin foil to allow the steam to escape, and leave to rest for 1 minute.

5 Then, unwrap the beetroot, roughly chop, and place in a food processor.

6 Add in 1 tablespoon of water, 1 tablespoon of balsamic vinegar, a pinch of sea salt and black pepper, and blend until smooth.

7 If it's still a little thick, add in a splash more water to thin out to your preferred consistency.

8 Place the salad leaves into a bowl with the chopped cucumber and onion, and toss well. Spoon in the pomegranate seeds, then drizzle over some of the dressing.

9 Toss the salad well and serve with the remaining dressing on the side to add as required.

WHAT YOU'LL NEED FROM YOUR STORE CUPBOARD
•Balsamic vinegar•Sea salt & black pepper

SUPER TOMATO SALAD

V5

5 Ingredients

- 125g/4oz cherry tomatoes, halved
- 75g/3oz sundried tomatoes, chopped
- 100g/3½oz rocket leaves
- 1 salad tomato, sliced
- 50g/2oz cucumber, chopped

Method

1 Place 4 of the chopped cherry tomatoes into a bowl and pour in 1 tablespoon of olive oil.

2 Using a pestle, or the end of a rolling pin, bash the tomatoes down to a lumpy mixture.

3 Season with sea salt and black pepper and add in a splash of lemon juice. Mix well and set aside.

4 Add the remaining cherry tomatoes and sundried tomatoes to a bowl, along with the rocket leaves.

5 Add in the cucumber and some of the tomato oil dressing, then toss well.

6 Serve the salad on a plate and arrange the sliced salad tomato on top.

7 Drizzle over some more of the prepared tomato oil dressing and serve.

WHAT YOU'LL NEED FROM YOUR STORE CUPBOARD
•Olive oil•Sea salt and black pepper
•Lemon juice

FRESH ORANGE AND FENNEL SALAD

V5

5 Ingredients

- 1 orange, halved
- ½ onion, peeled and chopped
- 1 small fennel bulb, finely chopped
- 100g/3½oz rocket leaves
- 1 tbsp pumpkin seeds

Method

1 Squeeze 1 teaspoon of fresh juice from half of the orange into a bowl, then add in ½ tablespoon of olive oil, a pinch of sea salt and black pepper, then set aside.

2 Add the chopped onion and fennel to a bowl with a pinch of freshly minced garlic and ½ teaspoon of finely grated orange zest.

3 Add in the rocket leaves and pumpkin seeds, and toss well.

4 Drizzle in some of the prepared orange dressing, toss the salad once more and tip into a shallow serving bowl..

5 Peel the remaining half of the orange and arrange the segments, still whole, on top of the salad. Serve with the remaining orange dressing to the side to add as desired.

WHAT YOU'LL NEED FROM YOUR STORE CUPBOARD
•Olive oil•Sea salt & black pepper

APPLE AND MAPLE MINT SALAD

V5

5 Ingredients

- 1 handful fresh mint leaves, finely choped
- 1 tsp maple syrup
- 1 gala apple, cored and sliced
- 50g/2oz baby leaf salad
- 1 tbsp pomegranate seeds

Method

1 Place the mint leaves into a pestle and mortar along with the maple syrup, 1 tablespoon of olive oil, a pinch of black pepper, a splash of lemon juice, a splash of balsamic vinegar, a splash of water and grind to create a dressing.

2 Place the salad leaves into a bowl, drizzle in some of the mint dressing, and toss well.

3 Add in the apple slices and pomegranate seeds, then toss well once more.

4 Drizzle over a little more dressing and serve.

WHAT YOU'LL NEED FROM YOUR STORE CUPBOARD

•Olive oil•Black pepper•Lemon juice
•Balsamic vinegar

GREEK TOFU SALAD

V5

5 Ingredients

- 150g/5oz firm tofu, diced
- 75g/3oz cucumber, quartered and sliced
- ½ red onion, peeled and chopped
- 75g/3oz cherry tomatoes, halved
- 50g/2oz mixed pitted olives, halved

Method

1 Place a pan on a medium heat and add in a drizzle of olive oil.

2 Dab the tofu with some kitchen towel to remove any excess moisture water, then place into the pan.

3 Cook for 7-10 minutes, turning the tofu half way through, until it is a light golden colour.

4 Meanwhile, place the cucumber, red onion, tomatoes and olives into a bowl and toss well.

5 Use some of the excess oil from the olives to coat the salad, add in a splash of lemon juice and season with black pepper.

6 Once cooked, add in the tofu from the pan, toss well once more, and serve.

WHAT YOU'LL NEED FROM YOUR STORE CUPBOARD
•Olive oil•Lemon juice

LIGHT BITES
AND
Sides

V5

BLACK BEAN NACHOS

V5

5 Ingredients

- 425g/15oz tinned black beans, drained and rinsed
- 450g/1lb tortilla chips
- 125g/4oz dairy-free cheese, grated
- 150g/5oz guacamole
- 150g/5oz salsa

Method

1 Preheat the oven to 350F/180C/Gas Mark 4.

2 Place a small saucepan on a medium heat and add in the black beans, along with a pinch of sea salt and black pepper.

3 Warm the beans through for 3-4 minutes, then set aside.

4 Arrange the tortilla chips on a large serving plate and top with the black beans.

5 Sprinkle over the cheese and place in the oven for 4-5 minutes, until the cheese is mostly melted.

6 Top with the guacamole and salsa, and serve.

WHAT YOU'LL NEED FROM YOUR STORE CUPBOARD
- Sea salt & black pepper

SESAME CAULIFLOWER STEAKS

V5

5 Ingredients

- 1 cauliflower head, cut lengthways into 4 'steaks'
- 1 tsp dried chilli flakes
- 4 tbsp dairy-free breadcrumbs
- 1 tsp sesame seeds
- 1 tsp paprika

Method

1 Preheat the oven to 200C/400F/Gas Mark 6 and line a baking tray with greaseproof paper.

2 Place the cauliflower steaks onto the baking tray.

3 Mix 4 tablespoons of olive oil, 2 teaspoons of lemon juice, 2 cloves of minced garlic, the chilli flakes, paprika, and a pinch of sea salt and black pepper together in a small bowl.

4 Use a brush to coat the cauliflower with half of the oil mixture, ensuring an even coating.

5 Place the cauliflower steaks in the oven to roast for 10 minutes.

6 Turn the steaks over gently, coat with the rest of the oil, top with the breadcrumbs then place them back in the oven.

7 Roast for a further 15 minutes, or until golden and tender.

8 To serve, place on individual plates, sprinkle over some sesame seeds and enjoy warm.

WHAT YOU'LL NEED FROM YOUR STORE CUPBOARD
•Olive oil•Lemon juice•Garlic
•Sea salt & black pepper

VEGETABLE TEMPURA

V5

5 Ingredients

- 1 small sweet potato, peeled
- 2 courgettes
- 1 carrot, peeled
- 1 tbsp corn starch
- 1 large cauliflower head, cut into florets

Method

1 Preheat a large saucepan over high heat and bring 1 Litre/32floz of vegetable oil to the boil.

2 Meanwhile, prepare the sweet potato, courgette and carrot by cutting them into matchsticks about ½cm each in width.

3 Place the corn starch into a bowl, along with 165g/5½oz plain flour, 1 teaspoon of baking powder, a pinch of sea salt and 150ml/5floz of cold water.

4 Whisk the mixture together until there is a reasonably smooth batter mixture.

5 In batches, place the vegetables into the batter, and then into the boiling oil. Don't put in too many at a time as otherwise the oil will cool slightly.

6 Cook for 2 minutes, until they become crispy, then remove with a slotted spoon and place on some kitchen towel to get rid of any excess oil.

7 Once all the vegetables have been cooked, serve immediately on a large serving dish and enjoy warm.

WHAT YOU'LL NEED FROM YOUR STORE CUPBOARD
•Vegetable oil•Baking powder •Sea salt •Plain flour

SIMPLY ORIGINAL HUMMUS & PITTA

V5

5 Ingredients

- 425g/15oz tinned chickpeas, drained & rinsed
- 2 tbsp tahini
- 1 tsp sesame seeds
- 4 pitta breads, cut into fingers
- 4 black olives, finely sliced

Method

1 Add the chickpeas and 2 tablespoons of lemon juice to a food blender.

2 Mince 1 clove of garlic and add to the blender, along with 3 tablespoons of olive oil, the tahini, a pinch of sea salt and 1 teaspoon of paprika.

3 Blitz the ingredients together until a creamy and smooth consistency is achieved.

4 If it is a little thick, add in a dash of water to your liking.

5 To serve, spoon into a sharing bowl, dust over some paprika and sprinkle the sesame seeds on top.

6 Add the finely sliced olives to the top. Place the bowl on the table and use the pitta bread fingers to dip in and enjoy.

WHAT YOU'LL NEED FROM YOUR STORE CUPBOARD
•Lemon juice•Garlic •Olive oil
•Sea salt •Paprika

TOMATO AND BASIL BRUSCHETTA

V5

5 Ingredients

- 12 slices Ciabatta
- 6 large salad tomatoes, chopped
- 1 small red onion, peeled and chopped
- 1 handful fresh basil, chopped
- 1 handful sliced black olives

Method

1 Preheat the grill to a medium high heat and line a baking tray with greaseproof paper.

2 Place the ciabatta slices onto the baking tray and brush each side a little olive oil.

3 Place the ciabatta under the grill for around 3-4 minutes on each side, until lightly browned.

4 Meanwhile add the chopped tomatoes into a bowl, along with the red onion.

5 Crush 1 garlic clove and add to the tomato mixture.

6 Next, add in the basil, 1 tablespoon of olive oil, ½ a teaspoon of balsamic vinegar, and season with sea salt and black pepper.

7 Once the ciabatta is toasted, place them onto a large serving plate and spoon on the tomato topping.

8 To serve, drizzle over a little olive oil and sprinkle with sliced black olives.

WHAT YOU'LL NEED FROM YOUR STORE CUPBOARD
- Olive oil • Garlic • Balsamic vinegar
- Sea salt & black pepper

TOFU SATAY SKEWERS

V5

5 Ingredients

- 3 tbsp smooth peanut butter
- 1 tsp soy sauce
- 1 lime
- 200g/7oz firm tofu, diced
- 1 tbsp roasted peanuts

Method

1 Spoon the peanut butter into a bowl.

2 Add in the soy sauce, the juice of ½ the lime, 1 freshly minced clove of garlic and 60ml/2floz of water.

3 Mix the ingredients together, then pour half the mixture into a roasting tin, setting the rest aside.

4 Place the tofu chunks in the roasting tin to marinate in the satay for 15 minutes.

5 Meanwhile, preheat the grill to a high setting.

6 Thread the marinated tofu onto four metal skewers, then place them on a baking tray and grill for 3-4 minutes on each side, until browned and crisp.

7 To serve, place the skewers on individual plates and drizzle over the remaining satay sauce.

8 Sprinkle over the roasted peanuts to serve with a wedge of lime on the side.

WHAT YOU'LL NEED FROM YOUR STORE CUPBOARD
- Garlic

RAW RAINBOW RICE PAPER ROLLS

V5

5 Ingredients

- 6 sheets of rice paper
- 4 small carrots, peeled
- 100g/3½ purple cabbage
- 1 cucumber
- 4 spring onions, finely sliced

Method

1 Cut the carrots, purple cabbage and cucumber into thin strips.

2 Dip the rice papers into a shallow bowl filled with water until they are slightly wet on both sides, but don't let them get too soft.

3 Arrange the vegetables in the centre of the rice papers.

4 Carefully roll them up, similar to a burrito, folding in the edges, and serve.

CHEF'S NOTE
You can add any of your favourite vegetables to this recipe and they taste great with a peanut dipping sauce.

BBQ CAULIFLOWER BITES

V5

5 Ingredients

- 2 large cauliflower heads, cut into florets
- 200ml/7floz cup almond milk, unsweetened
- 175g/6oz plain flour
- 175g/6oz breadcrumbs
- 225g/8oz vegan BBQ sauce

Method

1 Preheat the oven to 350F/180C/Gas Mark 4 and line a baking tray with greaseproof paper.

2 Place the plain flour in a bowl, then pour in the almond milk and 60ml/2floz of cold water.

3 Add in 1 minced clove of garlic, 2 teaspoons of paprika and a pinch of salt and black pepper.

4 Stir the mixture thoroughly to create a smooth batter.

5 Next, dip the cauliflower florets into the batter, ensuring an even coating.

6 Roll the florets in the breadcrumbs and place them onto the baking tray.

7 Cook for 10 minutes, until lightly golden and crispy.

8 Transfer the cooked florets into large bowl and coat them with the BBQ sauce, stirring well.

9 Return the coated florets to the baking tray and cook for a further 15 minutes or until tender..

WHAT YOU'LL NEED FROM YOUR STORE CUPBOARD
Garlic•Paprika•Sea salt & Black pepper

LINSEED AND CHILLI TOMATOES ON TOAST

V5

5 Ingredients

- 1 red chilli, de-seeded and finely sliced
- 2 large slices wholegrain vegan bread
- 1 tsp dairy-free spread
- 1 tsp linseeds
- 1 tsp sunflower seeds

Method

1 Pour 200g/7oz tinned tomatoes into a pan on a medium heat.

2 Add in 1 clove of freshly minced garlic, a pinch of sea salt and black pepper, 1 teaspoon of tomato puree and the red chilli.

3 Stir well and allow the mixture to come to a simmer.

4 Add in 1 teaspoon of chilli powder, stir well, and allow to simmer for a further 4-5 minutes, reducing the heat if necessary so the mixture does not boil.

5 If the mixture is still quite watery, simmer for a further few minutes.

6 Meanwhile, toast the slices of bread and spread over the dairy-free spread.

7 Pour the tomato mixture over the toast and sprinkle over the seeds to serve.

WHAT YOU'LL NEED FROM YOUR STORE CUPBOARD

•Tinned tomatoes•Garlic•Sea salt & black pepper•Tomato puree•Chilli powder

CHICKPEA FRITTERS

V5

5 Ingredients

- 400g/14oz tinned chickpeas, drained and rinsed
- 1 large courgette, grated
- 4 tbsp chickpea flour
- 1 tbsp nutritional yeast
- 2 tsp paprika

Method

1 Preheat the oven to 350F/180C/Gas Mark 4.

2 Sprinkle some sea salt over the grated courgette, toss well and leave for 10 minutes.

3 Squeeze the water out of the courgettes and put them in a large bowl.

4 Meanwhile, sauté the chickpeas in a pan over a medium heat for 5 minutes, then mash with a potato masher before setting aside.

5 Add the mashed chickpeas, flour, nutritional yeast, paprika and 1 clove of freshly minced garlic to the courgette and mix together thoroughly.

6 Mould the mixture into patties using your hands, then place them on a large roasting tin.

7 Brush the fritters with coconut oil and cook for 10– minutes on each side, until they are golden brown, crispy and piping hot.

8 To serve, place on a large serving plate and dive in whilst they are still warm.

WHAT YOU'LL NEED FROM YOUR STORE CUPBOARD
•Sea salt & black pepper•Coconut oil
•Garlic

DAIRY-FREE MUSHROOM AND CHEESE OMELETTE

V5

5 Ingredients

- 25ml/1fl oz soya milk
- 15g/½oz chickpea flour
- A large pinch of turmeric
- 50g/2oz mushrooms, finely chopped
- 25g/1oz dairy-free cheese, grated

Method

1 Pour the soya milk, a splash of water and the flour into a bowl and mix well.

2 Add in a small clove of freshly minced garlic, the turmeric and a pinch of sea salt and black pepper to season.

3 Pour the mixture into a food processor and blend until a smooth, lump-free mixture is formed.

4 Pour the mixture back into the bowl and stir in the mushrooms and vegan cheese.

5 Warm a pan on a medium heat and drizzle in some olive oil.

6 Pour the mixture into the pan and cook for 2–3 minutes, or until the edges have begun to seal.

7 Carefully flip the omelette over to cook the other side for a further 2–3 minutes. and serve straight from the pan.

WHAT YOU'LL NEED FROM YOUR STORE CUPBOARD
•Water•Garlic•Salt and black pepper
•Olive oil

CAULIFLOWER & SUNFLOWER SEED HASH BROWNS

V5

5 Ingredients

- ½ cauliflower, cut into florets
- ½ onion, peeled and finely chopped
- 2 tbsp dairy-free breadcrumbs
- 25g/1oz yeast
- ½ tsp sunflower seeds

Method

1 Preheat the oven to 350F/180C/Gas Mark 4.

2 Place the cauliflower florets into a food processor and give them a quick pulse to create crumbs.

3 Transfer the cauliflower crumbs into a bowl.

4 Add in the chopped onion, breadcrumbs and yeast, along with ½ clove of freshly minced garlic, a pinch of sea salt and black pepper, and a splash of water.

5 Stir the mixture well, add in the sunflower seeds, then use your hands to firmly knead the mixture to combine well.

6 From the mixture, form either 4 large, or 6 smaller, balls and gently roll out into thick hash browns.

7 Drizzle over a little sunflower oil and then place the cauliflower hash browns on a baking tray.

8 Cook in the oven for 20 minutes, or until tender in the middle and starting to crisp on the edge, turning over half way through.

WHAT YOU'LL NEED FROM YOUR STORE CUPBOARD

- Garlic
- Sea salt & black pepper
- Sunflower oil

SPICED BUTTERNUT SQUASH SOUP

V5

5 Ingredients

- 600ml/1 pint organic vegetable stock
- 400g/14oz butternut squash, peeled and diced
- ½ onion, peeled and finely chopped
- 1 tsp fresh coriander, finely chopped
- 1 tsp red curry paste

Method

1 Bring the organic vegetable stock to boil in a pan.

2 Add the butternut squash and onion to the stock and boil for 10 minutes.

3 Stir in the red curry paste, 1 teaspoon of paprika, ½ teaspoon of mild chilli powder and a large pinch of sea salt.

4 Allow the soup to boil until the vegetables are cooked through and tender.

5 Transfer the soup to a food processor and blend until smooth.

6 Serve immediately, whilst still piping hot.

WHAT YOU'LL NEED FROM YOUR STORE CUPBOARD
•Paprika•Mild chilli powder•Sea salt

ALL DAY BREAKFAST

V5

5 Ingredients

- 4 cauliflower and sunflower seed hash browns (page 45)
- 4 vegan sausages
- 2 tomatoes, halved
- 50g/2oz mushrooms, chopped
- 1 tin baked beans

Method

1 Preheat the oven to 350F/180C/Gas Mark 4.

2 If making the cauliflower hash browns from fresh, see the Cauliflower and Sunflower Seed Hash Brown recipe on page 45.

3 If already prepared, put to one side to warm through in the oven.

4 Place the sausages on a baking tray and cook in the oven for 20 minutes or until cooked through.

5 5 minutes before the end, add the cauliflower hash browns to the oven to warm.

6 Meanwhile, place a pan on a medium heat and add in a splash of olive oil.

7 Add in the mushrooms with ½ clove of freshly minced garlic and a pinch of sea salt and black pepper, and fry for 3–4 minutes, stirring occasionally.

8 In a small saucepan, pour in the baked beans and heat for 3–4 minutes, stirring regularly.

9 Once cooked, serve all ingredients on a plate and enjoy.

WHAT YOU'LL NEED FROM YOUR STORE CUPBOARD

•Olive oil•Garlic•Sea salt & black pepper

SWEET POTATO FALAFEL

V5

5 Ingredients

- Soft flesh from 2 large cooked sweet potatoes
- 400g/14oz garbanzo beans, cooked and drained
- 1 tsp ground cumin
- ½ tsp fresh coriander, finely chopped
- 1 tsp mild chilli powder

Method

1 Pre-heat the oven to 400F/200C/Gas Mark 6.

2 Place the sweet potato flesh, garbanzo beans 2 tablespoons of plain flour, 2 cloves of freshly minced garlic, 1 teaspoon of mild chilli powder and 1 teaspoon of cumin in a food processor and whizz until a smooth, dough-like texture is formed.

3 Spoon out the mixture and roll into balls, no bigger than a golf ball.

4 Place the falafel balls onto a baking tray, spacing them out evenly.

5 Cook for 20–25 minutes, or until they are cooked through.

6 Remove from the oven and serve.

WHAT YOU'LL NEED FROM YOUR STORE CUPBOARD
•Olive oil•Sea salt•Plain flour •Garlic

GREEN LENTIL MINI 'MEATBALL' SKEWERS

V5

5 Ingredients

- 150g/5oz green lentils, cooked and drained
- 75g/3oz chickpeas, cooked and drained
- ½ onion, peeled and finely chopped
- 100g/3½oz cherry tomatoes, halved
- A handful of fresh basil leaves

Method

1 Pre-heat the oven to 350F/180C/Gas Mark 4.

2 Place the green lentils, chickpeas and onion into a food processor.

3 Add in 2 tablespoons of plain flour, 1 freshly minced clove of garlic and a small pinch of sea salt.

4 Pour in 2 tablespoons of sunflower oil, then blend until a smooth, dough-like texture is formed.

5 Spoon out the mixture, roll into small balls, and place on a baking tray lined with greaseproof paper.

6 Cook in the oven for 15-20 minutes or until cooked through.

7 Thread the lentil balls onto skewers, followed by a tomato half or basil leaf, alternating accordingly.

8 Serve with your choice of dipping sauce.

WHAT YOU'LL NEED FROM YOUR STORE CUPBOARD
•Garlic•Plain Flour•Sea salt
•Sunflower oil

SPICED ROAST POTATOES

V5

5 Ingredients

- 200g/7oz Maris Piper potatoes, peeled and cubed
- 1 tsp cayenne pepper
- 1 tsp oregano
- A pinch of fresh parsley, finely chopped

Method

1 Preheat the oven to 400F/200C/Gas Mark 6.

2 Bring a pan of water to boil and boil the cubed potatoes for 5-7 minutes so the edges begin to soften.

3 Meanwhile, place the cayenne pepper, oregano and parsley into a large bowl with 1 tablespoon of plain flour, 1 teaspoon of paprika, ½ teaspoon of mild chilli powder and a large pinch of sea salt and black pepper.

4 Mix the spices and flour together well, giving the bowl a good shake.

5 Drain the potatoes into a colander, shaking well.

6 Place the potatoes in the spiced flour, shake the bowl and mix well to ensure a fairly even coating.

7 Take the potatoes out of the seasoning and place on a roasting tray.

8 Drizzle over a little olive oil and roast in the oven 20 minutes or until crispy on the outside and tender on the inside.

WHAT YOU'LL NEED FROM YOUR STORE CUPBOARD

•Plain flour•Paprika•Mild chilli powder•Sea salt & black pepper•Olive oil

LENTILS, GRAINS AND
Pasta

CREAMY GARLIC AND MUSHROOM FARFALLE

V5

5 Ingredients

- 2 tbsp coconut cream
- 200g/7oz dried farfalle pasta
- 150g/5oz mushrooms, chopped
- 50g/2oz spinach
- 1 tbsp parmesan-style dairy-free cheese, grated

Method

1 Bring a pan of water to boil, add in the pasta with a pinch of salt and leave to simmer for 10-12 minutes.

2 Place another pan on a medium heat and drizzle in some coconut oil.

3 Add in 3 cloves of freshly minced garlic along with the chopped mushrooms.

4 Cook for 2-3 minutes so that the mushrooms turn slightly golden and soft, stirring often, then add in the spinach.

5 Stir well and cook for a further minute, so the spinach begins to soften and wilt.

6 Season with black pepper and sprinkle in the parmesan-style cheese. Once the cheese has melted, spoon in the coconut cream and mix well, reducing the heat slightly, allowing the mixture to warm through but not boil.

7 Once cooked, remove the pasta from the heat, drain, then return to the pan. Pour the creamy garlic and mushroom sauce over the pasta, mix well, then serve.

WHAT YOU'LL NEED FROM YOUR STORE CUPBOARD

•Sea salt & black pepper•Coconut oil•Garlic

GRILLED FREEKEH & PORTOBELLO MUSHROOMS

V5

5 Ingredients

- 150g/5oz freekeh, rinsed
- 50g/2oz onion, peeled and finely chopped
- 1 tsp fresh parsley, finely chopped
- 2 portobello mushrooms, stalks removed
- 50g/2oz dairy-free cheese, grated

Method

1 Bring a pan of water to boil, add in the freekeh and simmer for 15-20 minutes or until tender.

2 Meanwhile, place a pan on a medium heat and add in a drizzle of olive oil. Add in the chopped onion and a clove of freshly minced garlic. Sauté for 2-3 minutes, until they begin to soften. Remove from the heat and place into a bowl with the chopped parsley.

3 Once cooked, drain the freekeh, transfer it into the bowl with the onion and preheat the grill.

4 Mix the freekeh with the onion, add in 1 teaspoon of tomato puree and season with sea salt and black pepper, stirring well.

5 Then, spoon the freekeh mixture into the mushroom caps, using the back of a spoon to compress the freekeh down.

6 Once full, place under the grill for 3-4 minutes.

7 Remove from the grill, sprinkle over the cheese, and return for a further 2-3 minutes, or until the cheese is melted and the mushrooms are tender

8 Serve alongside any remaining freekeh.

WHAT YOU'LL NEED FROM YOUR STORE CUPBOARD

•Olive oil•Garlic•Tomato puree
•Sea salt & black pepper

SERVES 4

PLANT-BASED MAC 'N' CHEESE

V5

····· 5 Ingredients ·····

- 200g/7oz cashew nuts
- 2 tsp corn starch
- 2 tsp vegan Dijon mustard

- 450g/1lb macaroni pasta
- 450g/1lb frozen peas

····· Method ·····

1 Preheat a large saucepan of water and bring to the boil.

2 Add in the macaroni and peas and cook for 10–12 minutes or until tender..

3 Meanwhile, add 450ml/15½floz of hot water, the cashews, corn starch, 2 minced garlic cloves, 2 teaspoons of vinegar, and a pinch of salt and pepper, to a food processor.

4 Blitz for 1-2 minute, until you get a creamy consistency.

5 Drain the macaroni and peas, then return them to the saucepan.

6 Pour the cashew sauce over the pasta and stir thoroughly to combine.

7 To serve, spoon the pasta into individual bowls and immediately.

WHAT YOU'LL NEED FROM YOUR STORE CUPBOARD

•Sea salt & black Pepper•Garlic•Vinegar

SPINACH AND BEAN SPAGHETTI

V5

5 Ingredients

- 100g/3½oz spaghetti
- 1 large red onion, finely chopped
- 200g/7oz cherry tomatoes, halved
- 225g/8oz tinned kidney beans, rinsed and drained
- 165g/5½oz spinach, washed

Method

1 Bring a saucepan of water to boil, add in the spaghetti and a splash of olive oil, and cook for 10-12 minutes or until tender.

2 Pour a dash of oil into a large frying pan on a medium-high heat and fry the red onion, 2 minced garlic cloves and the cherry tomatoes, until the onion is golden and softened..

3 Add a spoonful of pasta water to the frying pan and stir in the beans until heated through.

4 Place the spinach into the spaghetti pan to wilt.

5 Drain the spaghetti and spinach, combine with the bean mixture, toss everything together and serve straight from the pan.

WHAT YOU'LL NEED FROM YOUR STORE CUPBOARD
•Olive oil •Garlic

NICE AND CREAMY QUINOA RISOTTO

V5

5 Ingredients

- 1 celery stick, finely chopped
- 25g/1oz mushrooms, chopped
- 150g/5oz quinoa, rinsed

- ½ tsp nutmeg
- 1 tbsp soya cream

Method

1 Warm the olive oil in a pan, add in the celery and cook for 4-5 minutes.

2 Add the chopped mushrooms to the pan and cook for a further 3-4 minutes, until the celery and mushrooms are softening. Remove from the heat and set aside.

3 Bring 300ml of water to boil in a saucepan, then add in the quinoa and simmer for 10-12 minutes along with the nutmeg, stirring regularly or until the quinoa is fully cooked and expanded. Drain off any excess water.

4 Mix in the mushrooms, celery and soya cream, allowing the quinoa mixture to warm it through before serving.

5 Warm through and serve.

WHAT YOU'LL NEED FROM YOUR STORE CUPBOARD
•Olive oil•Sea salt

CHILLI PENNE PASTA

V5

5 Ingredients

- 200g/7oz dried penne pasta
- 100g/3½oz cherry tomatoes, chopped
- 1 red chilli, de-seeded and finely sliced
- 100g/3½oz passata
- ½ tsp chilli flakes

Method

1 Bring a pan of water to boil. Add in the penne pasta, along with a small pinch of salt, and cook for 10-12 minutes or until tender.

2 Place the chopped tomatoes into a bowl and give them a gentle bashing with a pestle or the end of a rolling pin.

3 Next, place a pan on a medium heat and drizzle in some olive oil. Add in 1 clove of freshly minced garlic, the red chilli and the mashed tomatoes. Stir well and simmer for 1-2 minutes.

4 Pour in the passata and sprinkle in a pinch of black pepper, ½ teaspoon of chilli powder and the chilli flakes.

5 Stir well, reduce the heat to a lower temperature and allow to simmer for 5-6 minutes, so that the mixture reduces slightly.

6 Once cooked, drain the pasta and place in bowls or plates. Pour over the chilli tomato sauce and serve.

WHAT YOU'LL NEED FROM YOUR STORE CUPBOARD
•Salt & pepper •Olive oil •Garlic
•Chilli powder

STORE CUPBOARD PASTA ARRABBIATA

V5

5 Ingredients

- 200g/7oz dried fusilli pasta
- 1 hot red chilli, finely sliced
- A small handful fresh basil leaves
- 400g/14oz tinned chopped tomatoes
- Pinch of caster sugar

Method

1 Bring a pan of water to boil and add in the fusilli pasta with a small pinch of salt.

2 Cook for 10-12 minutes or until tender..

3 Meanwhile, place a pan on a medium heat and add in a dash of olive oil.

4 Add in 1 clove of freshly minced garlic, the red chilli, a pinch of black pepper and tinned chopped tomatoes, along with the caster sugar.

5 Tear up the basil leaves, add to the sauce, and stir well.

6 Allow the sauce to simmer for 4-5 minutes, reducing the heat, if necessary, to prevent it from boiling.

7 Once cooked, drain the pasta and return it to the pan. Pour over the chilli tomato sauce and stir well so the pasta is completely coated.

8 Garnish with any remaining basil leaves and serve.

WHAT YOU'LL NEED FROM YOUR STORE CUPBOARD

•Salt & pepper•Olive oil•Garlic

PLANT-BASED SPAGHETTI AND 'MEATBALLS'

V5

5 Ingredients

- 100g/3½oz red lentils, cooked and drained
- 50g/2oz chickpeas, cooked and drained
- ½ onion, peeled and finely chopped
- 175g/6oz dried spaghetti
- 1 tbsp fresh mixed herbs

Method

1 Pre-heat the oven to 350F/180C/Gas Mark 4. Place the lentils, chickpeas, onion and 2 cloves of garlic into a bowl and mix well.

2 Sieve in 2 tablespoons of plain flour and a pinch of salt, mix, then transfer into a food processor. Pour in 2 tablespoons of sunflower oil and blend until a smooth, dough-like texture is formed. Spoon out the mixture and roll into small, evenly sized balls.

3 Cover a baking tray with grease-proof paper, evenly space out the lentil balls on the tray and cook in the oven for 20–25 minutes or until cooked through.

4 Meanwhile bring a pan of water to boil, add in the spaghetti and boil for 10–12 minutes or until tender.

5 While the spaghetti cooks, pour 400g/14oz of tinned tomatoes into a saucepan. Add in 1 tablespoon of tomato puree and 1 teaspoon of paprika. Stir and allow the mixture to simmer on a low heat for 10 minutes, so that the mixture begins to thicken.

6 Once cooked, drain the spaghetti and place onto plates, ready to serve. Remove the cooked lentil balls from the oven and arrange on top of the spaghetti. Spoon the tomato mixture on top and serve.

WHAT YOU'LL NEED FROM YOUR STORE CUPBOARD

•Garlic•Plain Flour•Salt•Sunflower oil•
•Tinned tomatoes•Tomato puree•
•Chilli powder

CARROT AND BUTTERNUT SQUASH RED QUINOA

V5

5 Ingredients

- 100g/3½oz carrots, peeled and diced
- 100g/3½oz butternut squash, peeled and diced
- 150g/5oz red quinoa, rinsed
- ½ onion, peeled and finely chopped
- ½ tsp fresh coriander, finely chopped

Method

1 Preheat the oven to 400F/200C/Gas Mark 6.

2 Add the chopped carrots and butternut squash to a bowl. Drizzle in some olive oil, along with a pinch of sea salt and black pepper, and 1 clove of freshly minced garlic.

3 Toss the vegetable chunks well in the seasoning and place on a roasting tray to cook in the oven for 20-25 minutes or until tender.

4 Bring a pan of water to boil with twice as much water than quinoa, if not a little more, then add in the quinoa with a pinch of salt and the onion.

5 Simmer for 5-7 minutes, stirring regularly, or until the quinoa is fully cooked and expanded.

6 Drain any excess water and return the quinoa to the pan.

7 Add in 1 teaspoon of tomato puree and a pinch of paprika.

8 Stir through the quinoa to warm, then add in the cooked carrot and butternut squash from the oven. Stir well and serve with a sprinkle of coriander on top.

WHAT YOU'LL NEED FROM YOUR STORE CUPBOARD
•Olive oil•Sea salt & black pepper•Garlic•Tomato puree•Paprika

SWEET POTATO STEW

V5

5 Ingredients

- ½ onion, chopped
- 400g/14oz coconut milk
- 600g/1lb5oz sweet potatoes, diced
- 1 tsp turmeric
- ½ tsp mixed spice

Method

1 Preheat a large saucepan over medium heat, add in 1 tablespoon of olive oil, 4 minced cloves of garlic and the chopped onion, and fry for 2 to 3 minutes.

2 Pour in the coconut milk, 400g/14oz of tinned chopped tomatoes, the sweet potatoes, turmeric and mixed spice, and cook for 20 to 25 minutes, or until the sweet potatoes are cooked through.

3 Season to taste with salt and black pepper.

4 Once cooked, serve immediately into bowls and enjoy hot.

WHAT YOU'LL NEED FROM YOUR STORE CUPBOARD
•Olive oil•Garlic •Sea salt•Black pepper

MUSHROOM STROGANOFF AND WILD RICE

V5

5 Ingredients

- 150g/5oz wild rice
- ½ onion, peeled and finely chopped
- 125g/4oz button mushrooms, halved
- ½ tbsp wholegrain mustard
- 125g/4oz non-dairy soured cream

Method

1 Place a pan of water on a medium heat and once boiling, add in the wild rice to cook until tender.

2 Meanwhile, place a pan on a medium heat and add in a splash of coconut oil.

3 Add in the onion and chopped mushrooms, along with a clove of freshly minced garlic.Cook for 3-4 minutes, stirring regularly.

4 Spoon in the wholegrain mustard, season with salt and pepper, stir well, then pour in the non-dairy soured cream to make a stroganoff sauce.

5 Continue to stir until warmed through, but do not allow the mixture to bubble; reduce the heat if necessary.

6 Once cooked, drain the rice and spoon onto a plate.

7 Pour over the mushroom stroganoff sauce and serve.

WHAT YOU'LL NEED FROM YOUR STORE CUPBOARD
•Coconut oil•Garlic•Sea salt and pepper

RED LENTIL BALLS WITH WILD RICE

V5

5 Ingredients

- 100g/3½oz red lentils, cooked and drained
- 50g/2oz chickpeas, cooked and drained
- ½ red onion, peeled and finely chopped
- 150g/5oz wild rice
- 2 spring onions, finely chopped

Method

1 Pre-heat the oven to 350F/180C/Gas Mark 4.

2 Add the lentils, chickpeas, chopped onion and 2 cloves of garlic to a food processor, along with 2 tablespoons of plain flour and a pinch of salt. Pour in 2 tablespoons of olive oil, then blend until smooth. Spoon out the mixture and roll into small balls, Cover a baking tray with grease-proof paper and place the lentil balls on the tray, evenly spaced out. Cook in the oven for 20–25 minutes or until cooked through.

3 After 10 minutes, bring a pan of water to boil. Add in the rice and cook on a medium heat until tender.

4 While the rice cooks, pour 400g/14oz of tinned tomatoes into a saucepan, along with 1 tablespoon of tomato puree, 1 freshly minced clove of garlic and a large pinch of sea salt and pepper, stirring well.

5 Allow the mixture to simmer and reduce on a low heat for 8-10 minutes, stirring every few minutes. Once cooked, drain the rice and spoon onto plates.

6 Remove the cooked lentil balls from the oven and arrange on top of the rice, before pouring the tomato sauce on top.

7 Enjoy immediately whilst still warm.

WHAT YOU'LL NEED FROM YOUR STORE CUPBOARD

•Garlic•Plain Flour•Salt•Olive oil
•Tinned tomatoes•Tomato puree

SLOW-COOKED MIXED BEAN CHILLI

V5

5 Ingredients

- 1 onion, peeled and chopped
- 150ml/5floz organic vegetable stock
- 400g/14oz tinned mixed beans
- 400g/14oz tinned chopped tomatoes
- 1 tsp paprika

Method

1 Pre-heat the oven to 300F/150C/Gas Mark 2 or switch the slow cooker on low.

2 Place a pan on a medium heat and drizzle in some olive oil. Add in the onion and a clove of minced garlic, and cook for 3-4 minutes, until the onion begins to soften.

3 Remove from the pan and place in a casserole dish, or the slow cooker.

4 Next, add in the vegetable stock, tinned tomatoes, 2 teaspoons of chilli powder, paprika and season with sea salt and pepper.

5 Stir the mixture well and then add in the mixed beans.

6 Cover and cook in the oven for at least 2-3 hours, or in the slow cooker for 5-6 hours. Serve with crusty bread and dairy free yoghurt dolloped on top if you like.

WHAT YOU'LL NEED FROM YOUR STORE CUPBOARD
•Olive oil•Garlic•Chilli powder
•Sea salt & black pepper

DELICIOUSLY CLASSIC GREEN PESTO PASTA

V5

5 Ingredients

- 3 tbsp pine nuts
- 1 tbsp dairy-free parmesan-style cheese, grated
- 1 large bunch fresh basil, torn
- 2 large handfuls wholegrain fusilli pasta

Method

1 Add the pine nuts and basil into a food processor, along with 1 clove of minced garlic, 3 tablespoons of olive oil, ½ teaspoon of lemon juice a pinch of sea salt, and most of the grated parmesan.

2 Blend until a smooth, lump free mixture forms. Place in a bowl and set aside.

3 Bring a pan of water to boil, add in the pasta with a pinch of salt, and cook until tender.

4 Once cooked, drain the pasta and return to the pan on a low heat.

5 Spoon in the pesto pasta sauce and warm through, stirring continuously.

6 Serve straight from the pan and sprinkle the remaining parmesan-style cheese on top.

WHAT YOU'LL NEED FROM YOUR STORE CUPBOARD

•Garlic•Olive oil•Lemon juice•Sea salt

WARM MIXED RICE SALAD

V5

5 Ingredients

- 50g/2oz wholegrain rice
- 50g/2oz brown rice
- 50g/2oz wild rice
- 1 red pepper, de-seeded and chopped
- ½ red onion, peeled and chopped

Method

1 Bring a pan of water to boil over a medium heat and add in the mixed rice with a pinch of salt.

2 Allow the rice to boil for 15-20 minutes or until tender.

3 Meanwhile, place a pan on a medium heat and drizzle in some sunflower oil.

4 Add in the chopped pepper and onion, and cook for 5-7 minutes, until they begin to soften and crisp a little at the edges. Remove from the heat and place to one side.

5 Once cooked, drain the rice and return to the pan.

6 Add in 1 teaspoon of tomato puree, a dash of olive oil, a minced clove of garlic, a pinch of paprika and a pinch of black pepper.

7 Transfer the cooked onion and pepper from the pan into the rice and stir thoroughly.

8 Serve straight from the pan.

WHAT YOU'LL NEED FROM YOUR STORE CUPBOARD
•Salt•Black pepper•Sunflower oil
•Tomato puree•Olive oil•Garlic•Paprika

SUNDRIED TOMATO AND YELLOW PEPPER QUINOA

V5

5 Ingredients

- 200g/7oz quinoa, rinsed
- 125g/4oz sundried tomatoes, chopped
- 1 yellow pepper, de-seeded and chopped
- 25g/1oz pitted black olives, chopped
- 1 tsp fresh parsley, finely chopped

Method

1 Preheat the oven to 400F/200C/Gas Mark 6.

2 Pour 400ml/14floz of water into a pan, add in the rinsed quinoa, and bring to a boil.

3 Allow the quinoa to simmer for 12-15 minutes, stirring occasionally.

4 Meanwhile, place a pan on a medium heat and add in a drizzle of sunflower oil.

5 Add in the yellow pepper and cook for 5-6 minutes, stirring regularly, until tender and beginning to crisp.

6 Once cooked, drain the quinoa and set aside to cool for a few minutes.

7 Transfer the quinoa into a bowl, add in the cooked pepper and stir well.

8 Next, add in the chopped sundried tomatoes and olives, then stir well again.

9 Finally, add in a splash of lemon juice and the chopped parsley, stir a final time, and serve.

WHAT YOU'LL NEED FROM YOUR STORE CUPBOARD

- Sunflower oil

COURGETTE AND RED PEPPER FREEKEH

V5

5 Ingredients

- 100g/3½oz courgette, chopped
- 1 red pepper, de-seeded and chopped
- 1 small red onion, peeled and chopped
- 75g/3oz cherry tomatoes, halved
- 200g/7oz freekeh, rinsed

Method

1 Preheat the oven to 350F/180C/Gas Mark 4.

2 Place the chopped courgette, red pepper, red onion and cherry tomatoes into a roasting dish and drizzle over some olive oil.

3 Stir the vegetables into the oil, adding in a clove of freshly minced garlic and a large pinch of sea salt.

4 Cook in the oven for 20-25 minutes or until tender.

5 Meanwhile, bring a pan of water to boil. Add in the freekeh and simmer for 15–20 minutes or until tender.

6 Remove from the heat, drain any excess water, then place in a serving bowl.

7 Once cooked, transfer the roasted vegetables into the bowl of freekeh, add in ½ teaspoon of paprika, stir well and serve.

WHAT YOU'LL NEED FROM YOUR STORE CUPBOARD
•Olive oil•Garlic•Sea salt•Paprika

SPRING ONION AND RADISH WILD RICE

V5

5 Ingredients

- 200g/7oz wild rice
- 3 spring onions, finely sliced
- 1 radish, finely sliced
- A handful green sprouts
- 1 tbsp apple cider vinegar

Method

1 Bring a pan of water to boil, add in the wild rice and simmer for 15-20 minutes.

2 Meanwhile, place a small pan on a medium heat and add in a drizzle of sunflower oil.

3 Add in the chopped spring onions and radish, and sauté for 3-4 minutes, until they are beginning to soften, stirring regularly.

4 Once cooked, drain the wild rice and place into a serving bowl.

5 Remove the spring onion and radish from the heat and transfer into the bowl of wild rice.

6 Add in the green sprouts and mix well.

7 Pour in the apple cider vinegar and 1 tablespoon of lemon juice.

8 Sprinkle in a small pinch of black pepper, mix well, then serve.

WHAT YOU'LL NEED FROM YOUR STORE CUPBOARD

•Sunflower oil•Lemon juice•Black pepper

SWEET POTATO CURRY WITH BROWN RICE

V5

5 Ingredients

- 200g/7oz cooked sweet potatoes, peeled and diced
- ½ onion, peeled and finely chopped
- 1 red chilli, finely sliced
- 1 tsp garam masala
- 150g/3½oz brown rice

Method

1 Preheat to 300F/150C/Gas Mark 2.

2 Pour into a casserole dish 400g/7oz tinned tomatoes and a pinch of salt and pepper. Add in the cooked sweet potatoes, onion and chilli, and stir well, covering the vegetables in the tomato sauce.. Add in the garam masala and 1 teaspoon of paprika.

3 cover with the lid and cook for 20-25 minutes or until piping hot (if you are not short of time cook for longer)..

4 Meanwhile bring a pan of water to boil and cook the rice with a pinch of salt until tender.

5 Drain the rice and top with the sweet potato curry.

WHAT YOU'LL NEED FROM YOUR STORE CUPBOARD
•Tinned tomatoes•Salt•Black pepper •Paprika

SUPER GREEN RISOTTO

V5

5 Ingredients

- 75g/3oz green beans, chopped
- 75g/3oz asparagus tips
- 150g/3½oz Arborio rice
- 250ml/8½floz organic vegetable stock
- 50g/2oz spinach

Method

1 Place a pan on a medium heat and add in ½ tablespoon of coconut oil.

2 Add in the green beans, asparagus tips and a generous pinch of salt.

3 Mince a clove of garlic, add to the pan, stir well, and allow the vegetables to sauté for 3-4 minutes, until they begin to soften.

4 Add the Arborio rice into the pan, stir well, and cook for 2-3 minutes so the rice begins to turn less translucent, stirring continuously.

5 Pour in a third of the vegetable stock, reduce the heat a little, and allow the rice and vegetables to simmer in the stock, stirring occasionally, until the stock has been completely absorbed by the rice.

6 Then, pour in another third of the vegetable stock and repeat this process.

7 Pour in the final third, whilst adding in the spinach, and repeat the process as before.

8 Once all of the stock is absorbed and the rice is cooked through, remove from the heat and serve.

WHAT YOU'LL NEED FROM YOUR STORE CUPBOARD
•Coconut oil•Sea salt•Garlic

ASPARAGUS & MACADAMIA WHOLEGRAIN RICE

V5

5 Ingredients

- 60g/2½oz macadamia nuts
- 150g/5oz wholegrain rice
- 75g/3oz asparagus tips

- 1 red pepper, de-seeded and chopped
- 25g/1oz button mushrooms, finely chopped

Method

1 Preheat the oven to 400F/200C/Gas Mark 6.

2 Scatter the macadamia nuts on a baking tray and roast in the oven for 7-8 minutes. Remove from the oven and set aside.

3 Bring a pan of water to boil, add in the rice with a pinch of salt, and simmer for 15-20 minutes or until tender.

4 Meanwhile, place a pan on a medium heat and add in 1 teaspoon of olive oil. Add in the asparagus tips, season with salt and black pepper, and cook for 3-4 minutes.

5 Add the red pepper into the pan, stir with the asparagus tips, and cook for a further 2-3 minutes.

6 Next, add in the chopped mushrooms and cook for a further 2-3 minutes.or until softened. Remove from the heat and set aside.

7 Once cooked, drain the rice and transfer into a bowl with a small splash of lemon juice.

8 Add the macadamia nuts into the rice, along with the cooked vegetables, collecting as much of the excess oil as possible, for flavour, stir well and serve.

WHAT YOU'LL NEED FROM YOUR STORE CUPBOARD

Sea salt•Black pepper•Olive oil •Lemon juice

PLANT
BASED
Desserts

V5

RICH AND RAW CHOCOLATE MINI PUDDINGS

V5

5 Ingredients

- 375ml/12floz tinned coconut cream
- 50g/2oz raw cacao powder
- 6 tbsp maple syrup
- ½ tsp desiccated coconut
- A small handful cacao nibs

Method

1 Place a pan on a low heat and add in the coconut cream, cacao powder and maple syrup.

2 Gently stir the mixture together for 2-3 minutes until it has a smooth, silky texture.

3 Cook for a further 2 minutes, stirring continuously.

4 Remove the saucepan from heat, stir in 2 teaspoons of vanilla extract, the desiccated coconut and a pinch of salt.

5 Pour the mixture across six ramekin dishes, cover, and refrigerate until set.

6 Once set, dust with a little cacao powder, sprinkle some cacao nibs over the top, and enjoy.

WHAT YOU'LL NEED FROM YOUR STORE CUPBOARD
•Vanilla extract•Salt

DARK CHOCOLATE BANANA SPLIT

V5

5 Ingredients

- 10 pecan halves
- 1 small banana, peeled & halved lengthways
- 2 tbsp maple syrup
- 40g/1½oz dark chocolate
- 1 scoop dairy-free vanilla ice cream

Method

1 Place a frying pan on a medium heat.

2 Add the pecans into the pan, lightly toast for 4-5 minutes, then set aside to cool on a plate.

3 Pour the maple syrup into the frying pan and place the banana in the syrup, cut-side down.

4 Caramelise the banana for 4-5 minutes, regularly spooning the syrup back over the banana.

5 Meanwhile, place the dark chocolate in a bowl and microwave for 30-40 seconds, or until melted.

6 Add ½ a teaspoon of salt to the chocolate and gently stir.

7 Place the caramelised bananas onto a plate, drizzle over the dark chocolate, sprinkle on the toasted pecan nuts and serve with a scoop of dairy free ice cream.

WHAT YOU'LL NEED FROM YOUR STORE CUPBOARD
- Salt

FIVE-FRUIT SALAD

V5

5 Ingredients

- 150g/5oz mango, peeled and diced
- 300g/11oz melon, peeled and diced
- 250g/9oz kiwi, peeled and sliced
- 1 lemon
- 200g/7oz blueberries

Method

1 Place the bite-sized chunks of mango and melon into a bowl, along with the kiwi.

2 Toss well together, allowing the fruit to soften slightly.

3 Sprinkle in some freshly grated zest from the lemon and stir.

4 Next, squeeze in the juice of the lemon and stir once more, coating the fruit in the fresh juice.

5 Add in the blueberries and toss well before serving.

CHEF'S NOTE
This healthy dessert is loaded with healthy antioxidants

DAIRY-FREE ULTIMATE CHOCOLATE BROWNIES

V5

5 Ingredients

- 100g/3½oz dairy-free dark chocolate chunks
- 100g/3½oz dairy-free milk chocolate chunks
- 180g/6½oz caster sugar
- 3 tbsp cocoa powder
- 250ml/8½floz unsweetened almond milk

Method

1 Preheat the oven to 180C/350F/Gas Mark 4.

2 Line a baking tin, around 20cm, with greaseproof paper and rub a little oil around the sides.

3 Place half of the chocolate chunks into a bowl and microwave for 30-40 seconds, or until melted, then set aside.

4 Sieve the cocoa powder and 175g/6oz self-raising flour into a large bowl, then add in a pinch of salt and thr caster sugar.

5 Mix together, then stir in 5 tablespoons of sunflower oil, the melted chocolate and almond milk.

6 Add the rest of the chocolate chunks into the mixture, stir well, and pour into the baking tin.

7 Cook in the oven for 20 minutes, or until cooked on the outside and gooey on the inside.

8 Once cooked, allow to cool on a wire rack for a few minutes before slicing and serving.

WHAT YOU'LL NEED FROM YOUR STORE CUPBOARD
- Self-raising flour
- Sunflower oil
- Salt

BERRY YOGHURT BOWL

V5

5 Ingredients

- 250g/9oz dairy-free coconut yoghurt
- 50g/2oz blueberries
- 50g/2oz raspberries
- 50g/2oz blackberries
- 50g/2oz cacao nibs

Method

1 Spoon the yoghurt into two separate bowls.

2 Wash the berries to remove any debris, then gently dry using some kitchen towel.

3 Place half of the berries into a bowl and gently mash with a fork.

4 Spoon the mashed berries into the bowls and stir into the yoghurt.

5 Sprinkle the remaining berries and cacao nibs on top to serve.

CHEF'S NOTE
Fresh berries make a great healthy dessert or an energy boosting on-the-go snack.

COCONUT COOKIES

V5

5 Ingredients

- 2 cups shredded unsweetened coconut
- 2 tbsp maple syrup
- 1 tbsp corn starch
- ½ tbsp coconut cream
- ½ tsp crushed almonds

Method

1 Pre-heat the oven to 190C/375F/Gas Mark 5 and line a baking tray with greaseproof paper.

2 Add the shredded coconut to a food processor and blitz for 1 minute, or until it begins to clump together.

3 Add in 2 tablespoons of coconut oil, the maple syrup, a pinch of sea salt and 1 teaspoon of vanilla extract, and blend for a further 30 seconds.

4 Next, add in the corn starch and coconut cream, and pulse until a wet dough forms; if the mixture is too dry, add a splash of water.

5 Use an ice-cream scoop to transfer the mixture onto the baking tray, making small mounds out of the dough.

6 Sprinkle some crushed almonds on top, then bake for 15 minutes, or until the tops are lightly golden.

7 Once cooked, cool on a wire rack before serving.

WHAT YOU'LL NEED FROM YOUR STORE CUPBOARD
•Coconut oil•Vanilla extract •Sea salt

BERRY AND AVOCADO ICES

V5

5 Ingredients

- 100g/3½ strawberries, chopped
- 50g/2oz blueberries
- 50g/2oz raspberries
- 1 large avocado, peeled, stoned and chopped
- 2 tsp maple syrup

Method

1 Place a small handful of the chopped strawberries to one side and then add the rest of the berries into a blender.

2 Add in the avocado, 1 teaspoon of vanilla extract and the maple syrup.

3 Blitz the mixture until smooth.

4 Pour the mixture into 4 small containers, cover with cling-film, and freeze for 30 minutes.

5 Remove from the freezer and allow the pots to soften for a few minutes before serving.

6 Scatter the remaining strawberries over the top and enjoy.

WHAT YOU'LL NEED FROM YOUR STORE CUPBOARD

- Vanilla extract

PEANUT BUTTER BANANA PANCAKES

V5

5 Ingredients

- 200g/7oz rolled oats
- 2 bananas, peeled and chopped
- 300ml/10½floz unsweetened soya milk
- 2 tbsp peanut butter
- A handful blueberries

Method

1 Pour the oats into a blender and blitz for 1 minute.

2 Add in the banana, along with 2 teaspoons of baking powder, 1 tablespoon of the peanut butter and the soya milk.

3 Blitz until the mixture is smooth.

4 Meanwhile, heat a non-stick frying pan on a medium heat.

5 In batches, pour the batter into the pan and fry for a couple of minutes on each side, until golden brown.

6 Meanwhile, place the remaining peanut butter into a small jug and microwave for around 30 seconds, until it becomes a runny sauce..

7 To serve, place the pancakes onto plates, scatter the blueberries on top and drizzle over the peanut butter sauce.

WHAT YOU'LL NEED FROM YOUR STORE CUPBOARD

- Baking powder

COCO-NUTTY ENERGY BALLS

V5

5 Ingredients

- 75g/3oz almonds
- 75g/3oz walnuts
- 175g/6oz Medjool dates, roughly chopped
- 40g/1½oz unsweetened cocoa powder
- 40g/1½oz coconut flakes

Method

1 Place the almonds and walnuts into a blender and blitz for 1 minute, stir, then blitz for a further 30 seconds, so a dough-like mixture begins to form.

2 Add in the dates, cocoa powder, half of the coconut flakes and a pinch of sea salt, and blend for 1-2 minutes.

3 Roll the dough into small balls, then roll each ball in the remaining coconut flakes.

4 Place on a tray and refrigerate for an hour before serving.

5 These bites can be stored in the fridge for up to a week in an airtight container.

WHAT YOU'LL NEED FROM YOUR STORE CUPBOARD
- Sea salt

FRUITY FLAPJACKS

V5

5 Ingredients

- 400g/14oz rolled porridge oats
- 250g/9oz mixed dried fruit
- 200g/7oz almond butter
- 200g/7oz golden syrup
- 200g/7oz soft brown sugar

Method

1 Preheat the oven to 160C/325F/Gas Mark 3 and line a 25cm baking tin with greaseproof paper.

2 In a large bowl, mix the oats and fruit together.

3 Place a pan on a low heat and spoon in the almond butter. Once the butter begins to melt, add in the golden syrup and brown sugar, stirring often until the mixture is smooth.

4 Add in the oats and stir thoroughly, ensuring an even coating.

5 Transfer the mixture into the baking tin and, once filled, press down gently on the flapjack with the back of a spoon to make sure it is level and compact.

6 Bake the flapjack for 20 minutes or until golden.

7 Once cooked, allow the tin to cool a little before cutting into slices.

8 Serve whilst still warm or prepare in advance and store in an airtight container until required.

CHEF'S NOTE
Flapjacks are great for maintaining energy levels. Try adding in nuts and seeds for extra protein.

NUTRITIONAL YEAST SEEDED POPCORN

V5

5 Ingredients

- 50g/2oz vegan nutritional yeast
- A pinch of cinnamon
- A pinch of nutmeg
- 125g/4oz popcorn kernels

Method

1 Mix 1 teaspoon of sea salt with the nutritional yeast, cinnamon and nutmeg in a large food container and set aside.

2 Heat a saucepan on a medium-high heat and add in 3 tablespoons of coconut oil.

3 Add a few kernels into the pan and once they begin to pop, add in the remaining kernels. Cover the pan with a lid and give the pan a good shake to ensure all kernels are coated in oil.

4 Then, as the kernels start to pop, shake the pan every 10-20 seconds.

5 When the popping slows, with just a few seconds between each pop, place the popcorn into the food container, cover with the lid and shake for 20 seconds, or until the popcorn is evenly coated.

6 To serve, place the popcorn into a large bowl and enjoy warm.

WHAT YOU'LL NEED FROM YOUR STORE CUPBOARD
• Sea salt • Coconut oil

SEA SALT AND MAPLE ENERGY BALLS

V5

5 Ingredients

- 100g/3½oz unsweetened shredded coconut
- 18 Medjool dates, pitted
- 100g/3½oz almonds
- 1 tbsp maple syrup

Method

1 Spoon a few tablespoons of the shredded coconut into a bowl and set aside.

2 Place the rest of the shredded coconut, dates, almonds, maple syrup and a pinch of salt into a blender and blitz for 2 minutes, until a dough-like mixture begins to form.

3 Roll the dough into 14 small round balls, then roll each ball in the remaining shredded coconut.

4 Place the balls onto a tray and refrigerate until firm.

WHAT YOU'LL NEED FROM YOUR STORE CUPBOARD
- Sea salt

CHIA SEED PUDDING

V5

5 Ingredients

- 6 tbsp chia seeds
- 2 cups unsweetened coconut milk
- 1 tbsp maple syrup
- A handful raspberries
- 1 tsp flaxseeds

Method

1 Place the chia seeds in a container and pour in the coconut milk.

2 Drizzle in the maple syrup, place the lid on the container, and shake well for 1 minute.

3 Give the mixture a stir, reseal and shake for a further minute, before placing in the fridge until the mixture thickens.

4 Split the pudding between two bowls, scatter over the raspberries and top with flaxseeds to serve.

CHEF'S NOTE
Chia seeds have numerous health benefits; they are high in omega-3 fatty acids, protein, and antioxidants.

RED BERRY COULIS

V5

5 Ingredients

- 1 tsp almond butter
- 50g/2oz raspberries
- 50g/2oz redcurrants
- 2 handfuls granola
- 150ml/5floz dairy-free yoghurt

Method

1 Place a pan on a medium heat.

2 Melt the almond butter in the pan, then add in the berries with a teaspoon of light brown sugar and stir well.

3 Reduce the heat and sauté for 4–5 minutes, stirring continuously.

4 Mash the berries with a spatula to help break them down and combine into a coulis style mixture.

5 Remove from the heat and set aside.

6 Add the granola into two bowls and then pour the dairy-free yoghurt on top.

7 Spoon over the red berry coulis and serve.

WHAT YOU'LL NEED FROM YOUR STORE CUPBOARD
- Light brown sugar

CINNAMON APPLE AND BLACKBERRY COMPOTE

V5

5 Ingredients

- 2 gala apples, peeled, cored and chopped
- A large pinch cinnamon
- 50g/2oz blackberries
- 1 tbsp maple syrup

Method

1 Place a pan on a medium heat and add in the chopped apples with ½ tablespoon of water.

2 Sprinkle in the cinnamon and a pinch of light brown sugar.

3 Sauté for 10 minutes, then add in the blackberries, stirring well.

4 Sauté for a further 10 minutes, then add in the maple syrup.

5 Mash the mixture down to create a smoother texture, then return to the heat for a final 5 minutes.

6 Enjoy whilst still warm or cool and store in the fridge to enjoy chilled later on.

WHAT YOU'LL NEED FROM YOUR STORE CUPBOARD
- Light brown sugar

RHUBARB AND APPLE CRUMBLE

V5

5 Ingredients

- 50g/2oz almond butter
- 125g/4oz rhubarb, washed and finely chopped
- 2 large cooking apples, peeled, cored and chopped
- ½ tsp ground cinnamon

Method

1 Pre-heat the oven to 350F/180C/Gas Mark 4.

2 Pour 75g/3oz plain flour into a bowl and add in the almond butter.

3 Add in 1 teaspoon of light brown sugar and stir.

4 Using your fingers, rub the mixture together to create a crumble.

5 Transfer the chopped rhubarb and apples into a small baking dish.

6 Sprinkle in 1 teaspoon of light brown sugar, along with the cinnamon, and mix well.

7 Sprinkle the crumble mixture on top of the apple and rhubarb until it is evenly covered.

8 Bake in the oven for 30-40 minutes, or until the crumble is golden and the fruit has softened.

WHAT YOU'LL NEED FROM YOUR STORE CUPBOARD

• Light brown sugar • Plain flour

TROPICAL FRUIT SALAD

V5

5 Ingredients

- 75g/3oz watermelon, peeled and chopped
- 75g/3oz mango, peeled and chopped
- 75g/3oz pineapple, peeled and chopped
- 2 tsp desiccated coconut

Method

1 Place the chopped watermelon onto some kitchen towel to remove a little of the excess water.

2 Then, place into a large bowl ready to serve.

3 Add in the chopped mango and pineapple and toss well together.

4 Add in a splash of lemon juice, the desiccated coconut and toss well once more.

5 Serve, or cover and place in the fridge to enjoy later on.

WHAT YOU'LL NEED FROM YOUR STORE CUPBOARD
- Lemon juice

COLD COCONUT CREAM PUDDING

V5

5 Ingredients

- 150ml/5floz coconut milk
- ½ tbsp maple syrup
- 60ml/2floz coconut cream
- A pinch desiccated coconut

Method

1 Pour the coconut milk into a food processor, along with the maple syrup and a splash of vanilla extract.

2 Give the mixture a stir before adding in the coconut cream.

3 Blend until completely smooth.

4 Pour the mixture into two ramekin dishes.

5 Place in the fridge and leave to cool and set.

6 Once set, remove from the fridge and sprinkle the desiccated coconut on top to serve.

WHAT YOU'LL NEED FROM YOUR STORE CUPBOARD
- Vanilla extract

SLOW-ROASTED CINNAMON PEAR

V5

5 Ingredients

- 2 pears, cored and halved
- 1 tbsp maple syrup
- ½ tsp cinnamon
- A pinch nutmeg
- 1 tsp crushed hazelnuts

Method

1 Pre-heat the oven to 325F/170C/Gas Mark 3.

2 Gently spoon out most of the pear from the centre, finely chop the pieces, then place into a bowl.

3 Mash the chopped pear as much as possible, then pour in the maple syrup, mixing well.

4 Mix in a pinch of brown sugar, along with the cinnamon and nutmeg.

5 Spoon the mixture back into the pear halves, pressing the mixture into the space.

6 Use any excess maple syrup to brush over the pear skins.

7 Roast in the oven for 20 minutes, or until golden and tender.

8 Sprinkle the hazelnuts on top to serve.

WHAT YOU'LL NEED FROM YOUR STORE CUPBOARD
- Light brown sugar

BLUEBERRY BUCKWHEAT MUFFINS

V5

5 Ingredients

- 100g/3½oz coconut sugar
- 2 tbsp almond butter
- 200ml/7floz almond milk
- 250g/9oz buckwheat flour
- 125g/4oz blueberries

Method

1 Preheat the oven to 350F/180C/Gas Mark 4.

2 In a bowl, combine the sugar and almond butter.

3 Pour in some of the almond milk, stir well, then begin to whisk the mixture.

4 Gradually pour in the rest of the milk, whisking continuously.

5 Sieve in the flour, along with 3 teaspoons of baking soda and a pinch of salt, and whisk well until a smooth mixture is created.

6 Mix in the blueberries, then spoon the mixture into muffin cases.

7 Bake in the oven for 15–20 minutes, or until cooked through.

WHAT YOU'LL NEED FROM YOUR STORE CUPBOARD
•Baking soda•Salt

BANANA AND WHITE CHOCOLATE LOAF

V5

5 Ingredients

- 3 tbsp cocoa butter
- 200ml/7floz almond milk
- 1 banana, peeled and sliced
- 40g/1½oz vegan white chocolate chunks
- 1 tsp crushed pecan nuts

Method

1 Preheat the oven to 350F/180C/Gas Mark 4 and line a loaf tin with grease-proof paper.

2 Spoon the butter into a bowl, add in 100g/3½oz caster sugar and mix well. Add a splash of vanilla extract and a third of the almond milk.

3 Whisk the ingredients together and, once a smooth mixture forms, begin to gradually pour in the rest of the milk, whisking well.

4 Gradually sieve in 3 tablespoons of baking soda and 225g/8oz plain flour, whisking the mixture well each time you add in a part of the flour.

5 Take half of the banana slices, chop them up into halves, and add into the mixture, along with the white chocolate chunks and half of the pecans.

6 Spoon the mixture into the loaf tin and top with the remaining banana slices and pecans.

7 Bake in the oven for 20 minutes, or until cooked through.

8 Remove from the oven and allow to cool before serving.

WHAT YOU'LL NEED FROM YOUR STORE CUPBOARD

•Caster sugar•Vanilla extract•Baking soda
•Plain flour

CONVERSION CHART: DRY INGREDIENTS

Metric	Imperial
7g	¼ oz
15g	½ oz
20g	¾ oz
25g	1 oz
40g	1½oz
50g	2oz
60g	2½oz
75g	3oz
100g	3½oz
125g	4oz
140g	4½oz
150g	5oz
165g	5½oz
175g	6oz
200g	7oz
225g	8oz
250g	9oz
275g	10oz
300g	11oz
350g	12oz
375g	13oz
400g	14oz

Metric	Imperial
425g	15oz
450g	1lb
500g	1lb 2oz
550g	1¼lb
600g	1lb 5oz
650g	1lb 7oz
675g	1½lb
700g	1lb 9oz
750g	1lb 11oz
800g	1¾lb
900g	2lb
1kg	2¼lb
1.1kg	2½lb
1.25kg	2¾lb
1.35kg	3lb
1.5kg	3lb 6oz
1.8kg	4lb
2kg	4½lb
2.25kg	5lb
2.5kg	5½lb
2.75kg	6lb

CONVERSION CHART: LIQUID MEASURES

Metric	Imperial	US
25ml	1fl oz	
60ml	2fl oz	¼ cup
75ml	2½ fl oz	
100ml	3½fl oz	
120ml	4fl oz	½ cup
150ml	5fl oz	
175ml	6fl oz	
200ml	7fl oz	
250ml	8½ fl oz	1 cup
300ml	10½ fl oz	
360ml	12½ fl oz	
400ml	14fl oz	
450ml	15½ fl oz	
600ml	1 pint	
750ml	1¼ pint	3 cups
1 litre	1½ pints	4 cups